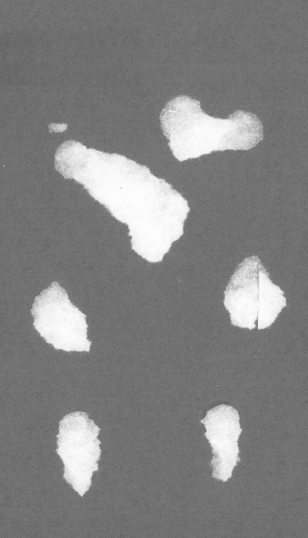

THE STRIPES AND STARS

THE EVOLUTION OF THE AMERICAN FLAG

By Boleslaw and Marie-Louise D'Otrange Mastai

AMON CARTER MUSEUM, FORT WORTH

The Amon Carter Museum was established in 1961 under the will of the late Amon G. Carter for the study and documentation of westering North America. The program of the Museum, expressed in publications, exhibitions, and permanent collections, reflects many aspects of American culture, both historic and contemporary.

LIBRARY OF CONGRESS CATALOG CARD NO. 73-87164 COPYRIGHT © 1973
ISBN 0-88360-001-3
AMON CARTER MUSEUM OF WESTERN ART. ALL RIGHTS RESERVED. LITHOGRAPHY IN USA

Contents

Acknowledgment

The occasion of the American Bicentennial observance is bringing to light many unusual documents, artistic and historic. In 1975-1976, American museums will focus on the significance of our cultural inheritance and their exhibitions will provide rich experience in the history of the arts in our nation.

Flags, particularly our national flags, seem an appropriate topic for the Amon Carter Museum's approach to this patriotic moment. Mrs. Mastai, author of the present text, with her husband, the collector of these historic flags, has pointed out the folk nature of the American flag—a national emblem, indeed, but for decades an emblem without legal definition which truly dwelt in the realm of popular art. Anyone could, and did, design a flag of his own choosing. The story of this metamorphosis of design is a fascinating revelation in the light of today's adherence to codes and practices involving use of and respect due to the flag.

The Museum is indebted to Ray Dryden and the Champlin Petroleum Company of Fort Worth for bringing the Mastai Collection to our attention. We are indebted to Alfred A. Knopf, Inc., publishers, for valued assistance in production of the color plates and permission to reproduce the chronology chart in the present catalogue. Finally, Marie-Louise and Boleslaw Mastai have given generously of their time and knowledge of the subject to prepare this gallery booklet. Through their untiring efforts, these national heirlooms have been preserved to record the evolving design of the stripes and stars. In a day when patriotism finds few outspoken adherents, the flag remains a changing yet constant symbol of the unity of the States, serving to remind us of our growing years.

Mitchell A. Wilder.

Chronology of the Flag

A LIST OF OFFICIAL AMERICAN FLAGS AND THEIR STARS*

Number of Flag	Number of Stars	Date Official	Original and Subsequent Additional States Represented, with Dates of Admission to Union
1st	13	June 14, 1777	The Original Thirteen Founding States DELAWARE; PENNSYLVANIA; NEW JERSEY; GEORGIA; CONNECTICUT; MASSACHUSETTS; MARYLAND; SOUTH CAROLINA; NEW HAMPSHIRE; VIRGINIA; NEW YORK; NORTH CAROLINA; RHODE ISLAND
2nd	15	May 1, 1795	VERMONT (March 4, 1791); KENTUCKY (June 1, 1792)
3rd	20	April 13, 1818	TENNESSEE (June 1, 1796); OHIO (February 19, 1803); LOUISIANA (April 30, 1812); INDIANA (December 11, 1816); MISSISSIPPI (December 10, 1817)
4th	21	July 4, 1819	ILLINOIS (December 3, 1818)
5th	23	July 4, 1820	ALABAMA (December 14, 1819); MAINE (March 15, 1820)
6th	24	July 4, 1822	MISSOURI (August 10, 1821)
7th	25	July 4, 1836	ARKANSAS (June 15, 1836)
8th	26	July 4, 1837	MICHIGAN (January 26, 1837)
9th	27	July 4, 1845	FLORIDA (March 3, 1845)
10th	28	July 4, 1846	TEXAS (December 29, 1845)
11th	29	July 4, 1847	IOWA (December 28, 1846)
12th	30	July 4, 1848	WISCONSIN (May 29, 1848)
13th	31	July 4, 1851	CALIFORNIA (September 9, 1850)
14th	32	July 4, 1858	MINNESOTA (May 11, 1858)
15th	33	July 4, 1859	OREGON (February 14, 1859)
16th	34	July 4, 1861	KANSAS (January 29, 1861)
17th	35	July 4, 1863	WEST VIRGINIA (June 20, 1863)
18th	36	July 4, 1865	NEVADA (October 31, 1864)
19th	37	July 4, 1867	NEBRASKA (March 1, 1867)
20th	38	July 4, 1877	COLORADO (August 1, 1876)
21st	43	July 4, 1890	NORTH DAKOTA (November 2, 1889); SOUTH DAKOTA (November 2, 1889); MONTANA (November 8, 1889); WASHINGTON (November 11, 1889); IDAHO, (July 3, 1890)
22nd	44	July 4, 1891	WYOMING (July 10, 1890)
23rd	45	July 4, 1896	UTAH (January 4, 1896)
24th	46	July 4, 1908	OKLAHOMA (November 16, 1907)
25th	48	July 4, 1912	NEW MEXICO (January 6, 1912); ARIZONA (February 14, 1912)
26th	49	July 4, 1959	ALASKA (January 3, 1959)
27th	50	July 4, 1960	HAWAII (August 21, 1959)

* Chronology courtesy of Alfred A. Knopf, Inc., New York City

President(s) Serving Under the Flag	War(s) in Which the Flag Was Used	Number of Flag
George Washington	War of Independence (1775-1783)	1st
George Washington; John Adams; Thomas Jefferson; James Madison; James Monroe	War with Barbary pirates (Tripoli war, (1801-1805); War of 1812 (1812-1815)	2nd
James Monroe		3rd
James Monroe		4th
James Monroe		5th
James Monroe; John Quincy Adams; Andrew Jackson		6th
Andrew Jackson, Martin Van Buren		7th
Martin Van Buren; William Henry Harrison; John Tyler; James K. Polk		8th
James K. Polk	Mexican War (1846-1848)	9th
James K. Polk	Mexican War	10th
James K. Polk	Mexican War	11th
James K. Polk; Zachary Taylor; Millard Fillmore		12th
Millard Fillmore; Franklin Pierce; James Buchanan		13th
James Buchanan		14th
James Buchanan; Abraham Lincoln	Civil War (1861-1865)	15th
Abraham Lincoln	Civil War	16th
Abraham Lincoln; Andrew Johnson	Civil War	17th
Andrew Johnson		18th
Andrew Johnson; Ulysses S. Grant; Rutherford B. Hayes		19th
Rutherford B. Hayes; James Garfield; Chester Alan Arthur; Grover Cleveland; Benjamin Harrison		20th
Benjamin Harrison		21st
Benjamin Harrison; Grover Cleveland		22nd
Grover Cleveland; William McKinley; Theodore Roosevelt	Spanish-American War (1898)	23rd
Theodore Roosevelt; William Howard Taft		24th
William Howard Taft; Woodrow Wilson; Warren G. Harding; Calvin Coolidge; Herbert Hoover; Franklin D. Roosevelt; Harry S. Truman; Dwight D. Eisenhower	World War I (1917-1918); World War II (1941-1945); Korean War (1950-1953)	25th
Dwight D. Eisenhower		26th
Dwight D. Eisenhower; John F. Kennedy; Lyndon B. Johnson; Richard M. Nixon	Vietnam War (1961-1973)	27th

The Stripes and Stars

During the first hundred years of our national history, generations of anonymous Americans graphically expressed their devotion to "the land of the free" by creating personal interpretations of "the flag of the free." No strictures of any kind had yet been placed on the fancy of patriotic flag-makers, and numerous design variants of "the stripes and stars," as the flag was first called, were flown simultaneously and with perfect legality by all citizens. This is a truly unique phenomenon, of which there is no equivalent in the history of any other national flag. As a result of this uninhibited freedom and imaginativeness, antique Stars and Stripes are national relics, precious historical and social documents of the American past whose abstract iconography constitutes an important manifestation of American folk art.

To view the flag from this entirely new aspect of design, however, calls for a different approach from the usual. It means, for instance, at the very start, complete exclusion of all the ancient banners planted on these shores by European explorers and colonists. The reason is not that such flags were not American in a national sense, but simply, in relation to our theme, that not one among them bears even the slightest design kinship to the future flag of stripes and stars.

Yet even if we rule out these flags of American prehistory, it will be found that the roots of the national emblem may still be traced back further than is generally realized. In respect to design, the distinction of a far-off precursor of the Stars and Stripes belongs in fact to a purely English banner: the "red ensign," which was floated on the ships of the first Anglo-Saxon colonists. This flag had a plain red field, and in the upper corner next to the staff a small white square (or "canton," the heraldic term) bearing the ancient device of England, the cross of St. George, also in red. Soon after their landing at Plymouth, however, the Pilgrims, in an upsurge of Puritan zeal, protested the use of this cross of St. George, which they denounced as "a remnant of popery." As a result, for a while "red ensigns" were flown in the Massachusetts Bay Colony with a totally blank canton: the red field as if ready to receive the white stripes, and the empty upper corner to welcome the future American constellation. Eventually the cross was reinstated, but its religious significance was neutralized by the addition of a worldly symbol—a small green tree emblematic of the sylvan wealth of New England. This first flag of New England not only related closely in composition to the Stars and Stripes to come, but was also the first prophetic indication of American independence of spirit. It was most appropriate, therefore, that a flag of this kind should have been—as historians now believe was indeed the case—among those flown at the battle of Bunker Hill.

THE REBELLIOUS STRIPES

American patriots had begun at least two decades earlier to organize for the protest that eventually grew into armed rebellion, and they had displayed "Liberty flags," so-called because the word LIBERTY was prominently figured on a field either white or of some solid color. There was one exception: the flag of the Sons of Liberty, a secret patriotic society, had its ground striped with nine vertical red and white stripes. The quantity nine was meant to represent "4/5,"—that of the famous pamphlet published in 1763 by the English statesman John Wilkes which played a role in fomenting the American Revolution. These first "rebellious stripes," as the British indignantly branded them, survive to this day in the familiar Coast Guard and Customs flags [2*] which have remained basically unchanged ever since the first "flag of the Revenue cutters" was established in 1799, with a field of 16 vertical stripes for the 16 states then forming the Union. The meaning of the cryptic number *nine* eventually became confused, or rather merged, with other allusions: the first rattlesnake as it appeared divided in *nine* sections in the Pennsylvania Gazette of 1754 (all New England states being represented by the head); and the fact that *nine* states had been first to ratify the Constitution. The number nine therefore came to signify the most fervent kind of patriotism, regardless of whether the stripes were horizontal or vertical [6].

*Reference numbers within brackets in boldface type indicate exhibition number and plate number herein; reference numbers within brackets not in boldface indicate exhibition number of flags not illustrated herein.

The striped flag of the Sons of Liberty was but one of a number of varied flags devised by the American patriots. The first recorded instance of horizontal stripes as emblem of the united colonies is found on the famous Markoe Flag—the regimental flag of the Philadelphia Troop of Light Horse, commanded by a Danish nobleman, Captain Abraham Markoe. The stripes are blue and silver and fill a small upper canton of the yellow silk flag. Blue and yellow are the Danish national colors, and the choice was hardly accidental.

FLAG OF COLONIAL UNION

The next significant appearance of the stripes involved not one regiment but the entire army assembled in Cambridge, Massachusetts, on January 1, 1776. On that occasion, a flag was raised which became variously known as the Grand Union, Great Union, Cambridge, Somerville, or Continental Flag [157]. Washington made use of the first name, and stated explicitly that the flag had been raised in honor "of the united colonies." It consisted of a field of 13 horizontal red and white stripes displaying in the canton the British union of crosses, a device combining the English cross of St. George with the cross of St. Andrew for Scotland. There is much uncertainty in regard to its origin, whether improvised on the spot by the troops, who added white stripes to their "red ensigns," or planned in advance by a Congressional committee. What matters to us is that the Grand Union Flag, during its official existence of almost a year and a half, established the national symbolism of the 13 horizontal stripes and tipped the scales at the psychological moment in favor of the combination of red and white. Other combinations are now forgotten: red and blue, yellow and white, yellow and black, white and blue, red and green, white and green—and even tricolor in "the colors of liberty," blue, red, and white.

The use of the American flag with tricolor stripes is recorded in contemporary pictorial records of the Dutch port of Texel. Here the fleet of John Paul Jones had anchored after the famous naval fight when the *Bonhomme Richard* "sank in victory" and the American admiral transferred to the captured *Serapis*. Jones had been accused of flamboyant eccentricity for his use of a tricolor striped American flag, and Benjamin Franklin and John Adams of carelessness for having stated in Europe that the American flag included tricolor stripes. Several European publications had been unjustly accused of inaccuracy for depicting such flags (for instance the Matthias Sprengel *Almanac* of 1784) [22]. According to a Connecticut chronicler of the period, even the Grand Union Flag may have been flown in a tricolor striped version. It was not until the discovery of the Texel records early in this century that the question was settled.

THE FIRST AMERICAN STARS

How and when did the stars, the second design element of the flag, come to join the American stripes? The earliest mention is found in some curious lines of a poem in the *Massachusetts Spy* on May 10, 1774, in commemoration of the Boston Massacre four years earlier:

A ray of bright glory now beams from afar,
The American ensign now sparkles a star,
Which shall shortly flame wide through the skies.

Was a star depicted on an American banner at this early date, or did some rallying flag shine *like* a star of hope for the patriots? Stars might have found a place on the flag because of their ancient meaning as beacons of hope, as well as symbols of man's highest aspirations.

Stars at that date were not represented by the five-pointed shape now familiar to us. They were then solely heraldic stars, which could never be less than six-pointed. The five-pointed shape was reserved for another heraldic device, the *molet,* or rowel of a spur, a recognized emblem of Christian chivalry already well known at the time the star proper was brought to Europe from the Orient by the Crusaders. Heraldic stars had figured as early as 1676 in some Rhode Island town seals. In 1780 when the Rhode Islanders wished to change the name of King County to Washington County, they chose as a new device for the county seal a *molet,* because this device formed part of the arms of the Washington family [8]. They differentiated this *molet* by picturing the central hole which is the axis of the spur.

Popular awareness of the proper appearance of a ''star'' is revealed in the charming, if apocryphal, tale of Betsy Ross. The seamstress of Philadelphia, as we all know, reputedly demonstrated to her illustrious visitors ''with a snip of her scissors,'' that a five-pointed shape would be far easier of execution than the six-pointed shape which had been indicated on the drawing from which she was to work. Betsy Ross was indeed a flag-maker, and she did make some early flags (though of what kind is not known). It is therefore possible that she made this ingenious suggestion. The earliest Stars and Stripes carried six-pointed heraldic stars (in some instances, seven- and eight-pointed), but this was soon changed to five-pointed ''American stars,'' as the *molets* eventually would become known, almost universally displacing the older symbol.

OUR FLAG IS BORN

In contrast to the Great Seal of the United States, no careful documentation of the development of the flag's design was kept before June 14, 1777. On that fateful date, a brief resolution of 29 words in the rough journal of Congress, kept by Secretary Charles Thompson, formulated the "birth certificate" of the flag:

> Resolved: That the Flag of the united states [sic] be
> 13 stripes alternate red and white, that the union be
> 13 stars in a blue field, representing a new constellation.

The simple grandeur of that statement marked it for the ages but furnished no information why the stripes and stars were chosen. The composition of the flag would, by implication, follow that of the Grand Union Flag. In regard to the stars, with no exact shape specified, the existing heraldic tradition would be followed at first, as well as another heraldic law relating juxtaposition of colors, so that some early Stars and Stripes have six-pointed stars and show the stripes in the white/red sequence.

The persistence of these ancient traditions may be traced through various examples as late as the eve of the Civil War. A memorial textile made in 1819 [153] after an American design of 1783 shows two large flags at the foot of a statue of Washington; one is the Stars and Stripes, the other the royal flag of France. This large American flag displays 13 stripes in the heraldic sequence, white/red. The canton, however, is white, on which six-pointed heraldic stars are indicated with the heraldic crosshatching denoting blue. Blue stars were not an uncommon feature in early American flugs. Like the blue and white stripes of regimental banners, they appear to have served primarily as militia colors (as in the "Blue Stars Flag") [9]. In a Victorian recreation of "The Hoisting of the Flag at the Battery in New York" (after the British evacuation), the great flag being unfurled is shown similarly with dark stars on a light canton and the white stripes appreciably wider than the red [12].

In the "Apotheosis of Benjamin Franklin and George Washington" of 1785 [1] also a monochrome textile, Indian heralds wave both the rattlesnake ensign and the American stripes in front of Washington's triumphal cart. Franklin ascends to Olympus guided by Minerva on whose buckler glow great fulgent stars of eight rays, characteristic of the treatment of heraldic stars in European art.

The mounting prestige of the American eagle as an element of patriotic design is revealed by its inclusion on a multistriped field of "American stripes" in two emblematic figures of America, dating respectively of 1798 [151] and 1800 [120]. By 1803, another version shows the Stars and

Stripes in somewhat more familiar guise [121]. In 1805, 15 flaming heraldic stars appear on the flag and jack in an engraving by J. Drake on a document signed by Thomas Jefferson [150]. Two great "eagle flags" of 26 stars date from 1838. The "Kingsboro Flag" [37] retains the heraldic sequence of white and red stripes. The other, the "Flag of the Washington Guards," [148] displays the six-pointed heraldic stars in flags on the front and, on the reverse, in the star-studded sky background behind the eagle. In the first book devoted to the history of the national flag, published in 1853, the flag then flown was represented with the union of stars in the shape of one great heraldic star of six points [41]. About 1850, a textile honoring George Washington displayed a halo of heraldic stars above the crossed flags and the medallion portrait of the Father of His Country. So highly appreciated and significant was this motif that it was chosen for inclusion on the "Know Nothing Flag," signed and dated 1858 [5]. A small paper flag of 33 stars [160] has not only six-pointed heraldic stars, but the red stripes are emphasized by thread-fine blue lines. Examples of heraldic stars, regimental stripes, and even tricolored stripes occur on illustrations to patriotic music sheets through this period.

THE NEW CONSTELLATION

In addition to the interplay of heraldic and popular elements, the variety of patterns for the placement of the stars leaves no doubt that the design of the Stars and Stripes was what might be called today a collaborative effort. There was only onc contemporary claim for authorship, that of Francis Hopkinson, one of the three Commissioners of the Continental Navy Board, who had already played a role in the designing of the seals of the Admiralty, the Treasury Board, and the Great Seal. Although his claim was not contested, he was denied the slight compensation he sought on the grounds that he had not been the only one to contribute to the design of the flag. It is now believed that Hopkinson in all likelihood was responsible for the version that became known as the "naval" pattern. This is known in heraldry as *semé* (literally, "seeded") and in textile designing as quincuncial, i.e., based on a group of five units. As placing of 13 stars in this fashion resulted also in a coincidental defining of the two British crosses [5] this pattern may not have been palatable to all patriots. Whether for this reason or any other, some early Stars and Stripes do have the stars in parallel rows, sometimes regularly [19] and at other times with complete disregard of symmetry [156].

The most familiar of all canton patterns of the Revolutionary period is the wreath of 13 stars of the so-called "Betsy Ross" pattern [134]. A ring of 12 stars with one star at center is also known to have been popular [15].

A flag of this type was carried at the Battle of Cowpens by the Third Maryland Regiment, with whom this pattern remains closely associated.

A Stars and Stripes with its stars set in a graceful oval pattern was depicted by the Franch artist Pierre L'Enfant (best known for his work on the plans of the city of Washington) in a handsome allegorical vignette which he designed for the first membership certificate of the Society of the Cincinnati. The L'Enfant illustration may have been the inspiration for an exquisite silk flag of superlative workmanship that duplicates the painter's concept in every detail [13]. Regrettably, many interesting flags have not survived, victims of their innate fragility and the fortunes of war. For example the ''Lyre Flag'' is known only by illustration and as referred to by Schuyler Hamilton in his *The History of the National Flag of the United States* [41].

On May 1, 1795, The Second Flag Act took effect, officially establishing the flag of 15 stars and 15 stripes. There had been considerable objection to this decision, however, and some members of the House advocated a permanent return instead to the flag of 13 stars and 13 stripes. This flag had been originally created for ''the united states'' [sic] and there was no good reason why it could not symbolize the union of all the states regardless of the increased number. Continuous alterations would only cause unnecessary expense and eventual impairment of the flag's integrity. The stars, it was predicted, would dwindle to mere dots and the stripes would turn into lines.

This advice was disregarded. The effect was not evident to all in the flag of 15 stripes and 15 stars. In fact, the Fort McHenry flag of 15 stars and 15 stripes inspired Francis Scott Key to hymn ''the broad stripes and bright stars'' of the ''Star-Spangled Banner.'' This is the only instance of a national flag's furnishing the subject of the national anthem. In naming the stripes ahead of the stars, Key was following an already established tradition: both the First and Second Flag Resolution mention the stripes before the stars, and the same phrasing is used in a patriotic song of the War of 1812. There is nothing fortuitous, nor is it due to the convenience of rhyme, that the repetition occurs again and again: ''the glorious Stripes and Stars,'' 1829; ''the gleaming stripes and stars,'' 1856; ''under the Stripes and American Star, the Stripes and Liberty's Star,'' 1861, and in that same year, the national ode by Harrison Millard, ''Flag of the Free,'' sang of ''our stripes and stars lov'd and honored by all.''

''THE STARRY FLOWER OF LIBERTY''

By 1818, the Union had grown to 20 states, and the problem of increase as reflected in the flag could no longer be ignored. The concern was not aesthetic but had to do chiefly with recognition factors under conditions of diminished visibility at sea. It was appropriate, therefore, that the design of a new flag should be entrusted to a naval officer, a hero of the war of Tripoli, Captain Samuel G. Reid. His advice was to revert to the flag of 13 stripes while continuing the practice of adding a new star to the canton for each new state. Captain Reid also suggested two patterns for the placement of the stars: the first one in parallel rows for the Navy [16] and another with the stars grouped in the form of one "Great Star" for use on land and by the merchant marine [44].

It is notable that the committee in charge of the project, while it accepted these propositions, was careful to stress its earnest wish to leave the arrangement of the stars to personal choice: "...whether in the form of one great luminary, or, in the words of the original Resolution of 1777 'representing a new constellation.'" With the passing of this Third Flag Act, an era opened that was to last approximately 60 years—that is, to the time of the first Centennial. It proved to be the golden age of American flag design.

The reign of the Great Star, characterized as one of the most beautiful and enduring incarnations of the flag, has been unaccountably blotted out of the national consciousness in modern times. In accordance with Captain Reid's suggestion, the first flag of 20 stars to fly over the Capitol was of the Great Star pattern. Although the new Act had specified that each new flag should go into service on July 4 following the date of admission of a new state (in this instance Mississippi, admitted as the 20th state on December 10, 1817), no one had the patience to wait until July 4, 1818. Thus, the prototype of the modern flag, with its permanent field of 13 stripes, was raised on April 13, 1818.

We do not know the exact appearance of this Great Star flag. It may have been a six-pointed heraldic star, even if composed of five-pointed stars, a pattern already familiar from use in the Great Seal. Here it appears above the head of the eagle, and is reproduced today on the reverse of the one dollar bill. It is significant that in 1852, Schuyler Hamilton, author of the first book on the American flag, chose to use as illustration of the then valid flag of 30 stars a six-pointed Great Star with its rays reaching out to the limits of the canton [41]. This choice indicates that the Great Star pattern was still prime favorite 32 years after its official acceptance.

Whether five- or six-pointed, Great Star flags, like full-blown white flowers, blossomed over the land. This was the age when "the white wings of our commerce" were speeding swiftly over the Seven Seas, taking with them "to the farthest islands of the seas," as Admiral George Henry Preble put it, the Great Star ensigns that had been assigned as the merchant marine's own. In the port of Salem a veritable galaxy of Great Star flags must have glittered above the forest of tall masts along the docks as well as over the buildings of the great shipyards. One little boy was just then growing up in the old port, who would in time become famed as savant, wit, and poet, Oliver Wendell Holmes. It is not the least of his many distinctions that he also bestowed on the flag of his country that loveliest of names, "the starry flower of liberty," inspired no doubt by memory of the Great Star flags of his childhood as much as by those that brightened the dark days of the Civil War.

Another famous appellation, "Old Glory," was coined by a Salem sea captain, William Driver, in 1831. This flag has stars set in regular rows, but Captain Driver felt free to set a personal mark on his beloved flag in the form of a cut-out design of an anchor appliqued in a corner of the canton. Such instances of rampant originality were by no means exceptional. Flags being by nature ephemeral, much has been lost to us, making what remains all the more precious.

THE STARS IN ORBIT

The examples that have survived allow us to distinguish that two stylistic currents of flag design existed side by side. One is the "classical" (of which [45] is exemplary). The other is the "avant-garde," which might also be called *kinetic* because it sought more specially "this very quality of motion" extolled in 1846 by John D. Long (later Secretary of the Navy) as the most admirable characteristic of the Stars and Stripes. It is certainly to a kinetic pioneer that we owe the creation of the great "Gildersleeve Meteor" of 26 stars [60]. The first owner of this striking flag proudly inscribed his name on the headband. He may also have been the creator of this unusual constellation. To some the design appears as a much elongated Great Star. Others construe it as a stylized human figure. However, the two stars set inexplicably close to each other at the end next to the staff would make it a double-headed figure in one instance, or a star with a blunted tip in the other, neither of which is likely to have been the intention. The design may represent a compass, which could indicate continued Masonic influence. It may be simply the most original and poetic interpretation of any of the directives for "a new constellation." The asymmetric trail of stars appears to rush across and beyond the limits of the canton with cosmic vehemence.

The Great Star could also affect more earthly guises, as where the stars are grouped so densely together as to suggest the compact shape of a subtropical star fish [42]. Flags of pentagonal pattern were a logical evolution of the Great Star, achieved by filling the open arms with more stars. Perhaps the most interesting development of the Great Star was that which led by gradual degrees to a flower-like pattern in place of a stellar shape. This culminated in the "Great Flower Flag" [155] where the rays or arms have become convex, or ogival, and have thus been transformed into true "petals."

This was a belated meeting of East and West, for when the Chinese had their first glimpse of the Stars and Stripes in 1798, they called it the "flower flag" or "the flag beautiful like a flower." It is easy to understand how the unfamiliar stellar devices might suggest a scattering or a wreath of white blossoms. Another embodiment of the concept occurs in the exceedingly complex "Umbels (or Snowflakes) Flag," with its unique clusters of stars, each cluster a miniature Great Star by itself [46]. In perfect contrast to this lyrical example, the metaphysical "Lincoln Mourning Star," [48] delicate yet severe, has its diamantine stars set in a perfect pentagram. In another instance, the asymmetric placing of stars of varying sizes brings lighthearted scintillation to the composition [43].

In addition to numerous variations on the theme of the Great Star, some of the earlier geometric patterns continued in favor, with necessary adaptations to the larger number of stars. A "square frame" formation had been popular at the end of the 18th century: it appears here on the flag of 15 stars and 15 stripes depicted on a high comb of the neo-classical period [21]. On a flag of 31 stars the "frame" of stars consists now of two rows instead of a single one [27]. This was continued as late as 1873, where the same composition is featured on the flag held by a figure of Columbia at the helm of a ship [28].

In the beautiful "Irvine Flag" [26] we may trace the development of an archaic and rare pattern in which the stars were first set to outline the cross of St. George. As the Great Star became a pentagon, the square-angled cross has become a "diamond" by the same expedient. This flag originally had 29 stars, and the later addition of four more stars to keep up with the progress of the Union has somewhat obscured the original design. As the additional stars differ appreciably in texture, workmanship, and slant from the original stars, it is possible to single them out, thus bringing out the basic diamond shape. The two flags of 33 stars used at Fort Sumter during the bombardment by the Confederate forces in 1861 were of the diamond pattern, with columns of stars on each side. The fact that the Irvine Flag originally had 29 stars demonstrates that the "diamond" was used as early as 1847.

The "Parentheses or Butterfly Flag" [52] is closely related in design to a flag, also of 33 stars, illustrated on the cover of the program of the inaugural ceremonies for President McKinley in 1897, pictured as much battle-worn and tattered. This implies that this flag had apparently played an important role in some events of the Civil War 36 years before. As the McKinley program flag lacks the triad of stars in each corner, it may have a better right to the title of "Parentheses Flag," while "Butterfly Flag" conveys something of the airy grace of this kindred pattern, with starry "wing tips" extending to each corner of the canton.

CIVIL WAR STRIPES AND BARS

The pattern predominant during the Civil War may be defined as the "phalanx" formation, because the stars are superimposed in parallel rows of frankly military order. At times, the monotony is relieved by the use of "leader" or "followers" or both: two or even three stars set either in advance or to the rear of their comrades-in-arms. Paradoxically, regimental flags were far less spartan in mood. Their stars were frequently set in circular [**63**] or oval wreaths, in ogives, arches, or other even more imaginative formations. The pair of flags used by General George Brinton McClellan [106 and **107**] not in the field but in the forum during his unsuccessful Presidential campaign against Lincoln, stand midway between the civilian and the military. The admirable motto, "God and My Country," is exquisitely embroidered in blue silk. Such inscriptions which the stripes irresistibly invite had not yet been condemned: regimental flags bore on each stripe the name of one battle in which the corps had participated. Another military practice, as in the McClellan flags or the beautiful "Great Starry 'L'" regimental swallow-tailed banner [**63**] was the use of gold stars in place of white. The practice is also heraldically correct, as gold can always be used as a replacement for any color. The stars on the McClellan flags are notable in that they are built up of five juxtaposed lozenges meeting at the apex.

Wartime enthusiasm led to extremes. Miniature flags were made and waved by children [**126, 127,** and **128**] or served as covers for needlebooks [87, **88,** and **89**] while the equivalent adult expression of faith in the right and might of the Union took the form of outsize flags over which groups of patriotic women toiled in unison. The mammoth flag floated over the central station of the Erie Railroad in New Jersey is the supreme example. The largest known Civil War flag extant, it duplicates the size of the original Star-Spangled Banner, being 45 feet long [59].

Meanwhile, the flag of the Confederacy, the Stars and Bars, had been decided upon in a contest where many models were submitted, most of these being variations on the theme of the Stars and Stripes and thus betraying a profound attachment to the American colors and to the venerable pattern of "the old flag" [**65** and **66**]. The Stars and Bars [**67** and **69**] was in fact so much like the Stars and Stripes that it soon led to confusion in battle. The second flag of the Confederacy featured the "Southern Cross," 13 stars in a blue saltire on a red field, and became famed, in one of its forms, as the "Battle Flag." Like their northern counterparts, the regimental banners of the South displayed mottoes, though none surely more impressive than that chosen by a regiment from Nashville, Tennessee [**68**]. The solemn motto "God Armeth the Patriot" had been borne previously by another Nashville troop during the Creek Indian Wars of 1813, but may hark back even further. It appears to relate to the "Appeal to Heaven" inscribed on the "Pine Tree Flag" of the Washington floating batteries.

CENTENNIAL STANDARDS

The flag of 37 stars remained in service until 1877 and was therefore not only the flag of our first Centennial in 1876, but also of the centenary of the birth of the flag on June 14, 1777. The outstanding contribution of the period to flag design is the noble pattern of the great "medallion" flags consisting of two concentric wreaths of stars. The inner circle represents the 13 founding states, and the outer one is composed of the number of stars representing the states that joined the Union during the first century of national existence. The two examples shown here provide an interesting demonstration of the profound differences brought about in a basic pattern by apparently minor factors. The double-wreath design [104] with a single star at center fits rather closely within a squarish canton, and the effect achieved is of brilliance, substance, and strength. The other "medallion" of stars has an open center and is placed on a more elongated canton [51] with the result that the individual stars appear proportionately smaller and more distant, as if glittering in the depths of space.

Both handsome designs may justifiably be looked upon as the apogee of American flag-making before the impending mechanization of the modern age. For, in addition to design considerations, the human element plays an important role. When a replica was made of the great "medallion" flag with a central star [104] to be used above the main gate of the Metropolitan Museum in New York, it was found that the charm of the original was not reflected in the machine-made copy. The stars had been monotonously duplicated; they were all precisely alike, while each hand-made star is as subtly different from its neighbor as each leaf on a tree. Similarly the varying angles at which these stars are positioned one by one on the original had also been ignored. All stars pointed to the center, so that the effect achieved was as of the spokes of a wheel instead of a living, pulsing corona. As always, the imponderable made the difference.

In addition to the creation of these giants, professional and amateur flag-makers vied with each other to express fittingly the national Centennial jubilation. New industrial processes had recently made possible more brilliant and complex effects than ever before, as well as mass production on a hitherto undreamed-of scale. The most characteristic of the flag patterns of this type was the global design, printed on glazed muslin, in a color combination not previously encountered, a very dark navy blue for the canton and a clear vermilion red for the stripes [**83**]. The greatest achievement among commemorative printed flags is the dazzling "pyrotechnic" model of the "1776-1876" flag [**73**] that also embodied a surprisingly subtle allusion. Both dates on the canton are composed each of the 38 stars, the number of stars in the flag inaugurated on July 4, 1877, thus adding up to the symbolic total of "76." The "International Flag" [**77**] shows the Stars and Stripes surrounded by a border of the flags of all the nations that participated in the Centennial celebrations. It was probably unknown to the anonymous designer of this model that the effect must have closely approximated that of "the flag of the calico makers" which was carried in the Federal processinn in 1798, consisting of the national flag surrounded by a border made of swatches of assorted calicoes. The great tradition of hand-make "personal" flags had not yet entirely relinquished, however, and was still proudly represented with such outstanding examples as the unique "Hour-Glass Flag" [55] whose starry saltire hints broadly of the "Southern Cross;" or the delightful "Four-Cornered Flag" [**27**] with its beguiling, merrily jouncing stars "like pretty maids all in a row."

THE FLAG IN DAILY LIFE

It has been said that the flag is "our sole emblem of fidelity." The great stained-glass clock dial centering a flag of 32 stars [91] is eloquently symbolical: the beloved emblem has stood from the very start at the core of American life, never absent from thought or, literally, from view. There is hardly one artifact or utensil that has not at some time been made to bear the semblance of the national flag: furniture, furnishings of every kind, personal clothing, games, book covers, and bookplates are represented in the cross-section included here.

Mention has already been made, in relation to certain aspects of the design elements of the flag, of some of these examples: certain commemorative textiles [**1, 5,** and 153]; the turtle-shell high comb, a true masterpiece of American folk-art [**21**]; some petit-point flags as needlebook covers [87]. Other characteristic examples produced during the first century of American national life are the Washington memorial panel of 1800, combining painting and chenille embroidery [124]; the cover of a seaman's chest [25]; a game board, circa 1835; and a neckerchief, circa 1860, printed in a delicate repeat pattern [86]. It is notable that, except for the last item, all these articles were home-designed as well as home-made. The same applies to much of what was produced during the Civil War. The "Monitor" hooked rug, for instance, is a unique conception: the famous armored vessel is shown dwarfed by the great ensign it bears, with its exuberantly "floral" pattern of stars [32].

By the time of the First Centennial, the cult of the flag had already begun to shift from the flag proper to its innumerable reproductions in the swiftly mushrooming popular press and in an enormous variety of graphic media: posters, music sheets, the new-fangled "postal cards," calendars, advertising and business cards. These new developments were popularized by the Philadelphia Exposition of 1876 with its main theme of American industry, the wide publicity it was given, and the myriads of souvenirs in which the patriotic element was naturally and appropriately stressed [79, **80,** and **81**]. The broad dissemination and easy availability of printed flags, generally of thin silk or glazed muslin, if it did much to fan patriotic fervor, also largely erased the need to create personal flags. At times, it is true, commercial designers had flashes of genius, such as the anonymous creator of the "Bad Kissingen Flag" [54] which is noteworthy on two counts. First, it displayed a charming pattern of "dancing stars" (an effect that was achieved by placing several rows of staggered stars within the boundaries of two regular files of stars at top and bottom). Secondly, it is exemplary of those "flaglets" which patriotic American tourists or students took on their travels, nostalgically displayed in some "home away from home," flaunted proudly on the glorious Fourth, and eventually inscribed with some personally memorable place and date, a practice that had not yet been outlawed.

Barring the inevitable exceptions, however, from then on the few sporadic efforts one still encounters generally tend to incorporate the flag itself as part of a decorative scheme rather than bringing forth new interpretations of the American constellation, which indeed was swiftly turning into a galaxy.

FLAG OF EMPIRE

Four states were admitted to the Union in 1889. One day before the legal date of inclusion of their stars on the flag, July 4, 1890, Idaho came in as the 43rd state. Then, to compound confusion, a week later Wyoming was admitted as the 44th state. Small wonder that flags of 39, 40, 41, and 42 stars continued to be used, albeit unofficial.

Sometimes the obsolete flags were put to practical and decorative use. A quilted coverlet [**97**] made of small 39-star flags stitched together shows on the reverse an equivalent number of Centennial commemorative flags. But if flags of 39 stars had been produced in abundance, in expectation that the Dakota Territory would form only one state, more restraint was exercised in regard to the flags of 40, 41, and 42 stars. The flag of 43 stars was to all practical purposes nonexistent, although it enjoyed "official" recognition for one year.

Five territories remained by 1891, waiting to be accepted as states. Not surprisingly, this feeling of expectancy discouraged efforts at flag designing, particularly when the Spanish War brought, in addition, the delicate question of overseas possessions. Would these also eventually become states? This instability is expressed appropriately in the patterns of staggered rows, frequently asymmetric, that were made to do for the flags of 45 and 46 stars.

This temporary state of affairs came to an end in 1912, when the flag of 48 stars came into being. This flag might indeed have been called, like the first flag of union of the American patriots, a "Continental Flag," and this time with absolute literalness as the empire of United States now extended "from sea to shining sea." The honor of supervising the creation of a suitable new design for the flag of 48 stars [139] which was to have an uninterrupted reign of 47 years, was tendered the "Hero of Manila", Admiral George Dewey, on whom symbolically fell the mantle of Captain Reid. A joint Army and Navy Board, headed by Admiral Dewey, decided in favor of a pattern of six even rows of eight stars, an exceedingly substantial and compact "phalanx." This also, for the first time, was a mandatory design and in the same year further executive orders were issued, prescribing the exact configuration of the national flag with proportions for width of stripes and diameters of stars. Exact color tints were not prescribed until 1934. A code of flag etiquette had been formulated ten years earlier by patriotic societies, and became federal law in 1942.

What was probably the last spurt of creative originality in American flag design also occurred in 1912. This was the short-lived "Peace Flag" created by Wayne Whipple [144], which was widely publicized with the blessing of the authorities and President Taft and actually produced and flown. The design combined both the Great Star and wreath patterns to achieve a visual resumé of American history: the central six-pointed Great Star of 13 stars, as it appears on the Great Seal; the great ring, or wreath, of 25 stars for the states admitted to the Union during the first century of the country's history; the 10 stars outside the circle standing for the 10 states admitted between 1876 and 1912.

The flag of 49 stars brought a reversal to the staggered rows in 1959. However, as Alaska had been admitted on January 3 of that year, and Hawaii came in as the 50th state on August 21 of the same year, the flag of 49 stars, like the flag of 43 stars, had but a hypothetical existence. But the flag of 50 stars was indeed born under a lucky star, or, perhaps one should say, a lucky moon. Its total of stars lends itself equally well to almost any pattern one might name. The official decision was in favor of the quincuncial arrangement, so that the flag that went to the moon carried the Americans' stars there in an enlargement—a multiplied projection—of the basic pattern of the glorious first flag of 13 stars and 13 stripes.

In the mid-20th century, the flag cult of old came to be replaced by what one might perhaps term a "flag obsession." The first inklings of this phenomenon appeared in the works of then avant-garde artists: Johns, Rauschenberg, Rivers, and others. The vein was very soon sensationalized and exploited commercially. Some of these performances were unobjectionable, others, deeply offensive not only to patriotic sentiments but to every canon of good taste. What is undeniable however is the tremendous popularity and all-pervasiveness of the flag theme, enduring to this day. Book jacket covers for instance, displaying the flag, either complete or in part, are legion. Clothing, furnishings, etc., have similarly reflected the theme, whether in a friendly or a hostile vein.

All of this, however, should be looked upon as a social manifestation rather than a genuine artistic movement. The representation of the flag as subject matter of painting and sculpture or in purely decorative themes is not a satisfactory substitute for creative flag design. Admittedly this pursuit has been hampered in modern times by the fact that the pattern and exact tints of the flag are now strictly regulated by law, down to the minutest details. As a result, it would seem as though aspiring American flag designers do not stand a chance anymore. It should be remembered, however, that these regulations apply only to the flag when used as a *national* symbol. It may be permissible to hope that the coming of our third century of national existence may yet bring, in our own days, a true renaissance of American "personal" flags, inspired by and rivaling the splendidly uninhibited examples of the past.

BOLESLAW and MARIE-LOUISE D'OTRANGE MASTAI

Amagansett, New York
June 14, 1973, "Flag Day"

Color Plates

9 *Revolutionary Blue Stars Flag,*
Hand-lettered band added for Presidential campaign of 1880.
c. 1780-90. Wool and cotton. 60 x 114 in.

Flag Reversal Modern rules call for illustrating or displaying the
American flag with the canton on the observer's left. However, such
rules cannot always be followed in showing *antique* American flags.
Some antique American flags, designed before the adoption of the flag
code, either have one surface considerably more finished than the
other, e.g., the Minerva Flag [**19**] or else bear an inscription
only on one side, e.g., 1776-1876 Centennial Flag [**73**].

16 *Twenty-Star Flag (Detail).* 1818. Bunting. 57½ x 104 in.

17 *Hubbard Flag of 17 Stars, 13 Stripes.* 1803. Bunting. 32 x 48 in.

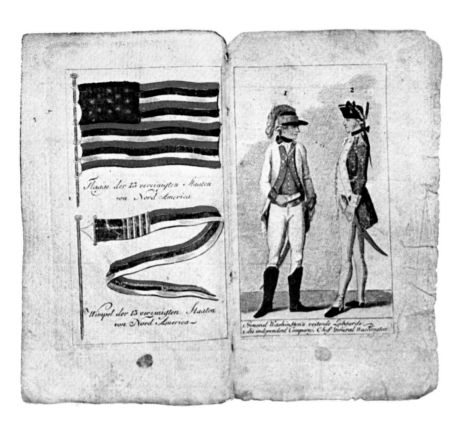

22 Matthias Sprengel, *Pocket Book Almanac*. 1784. Book. 5 x 3⅛ in.

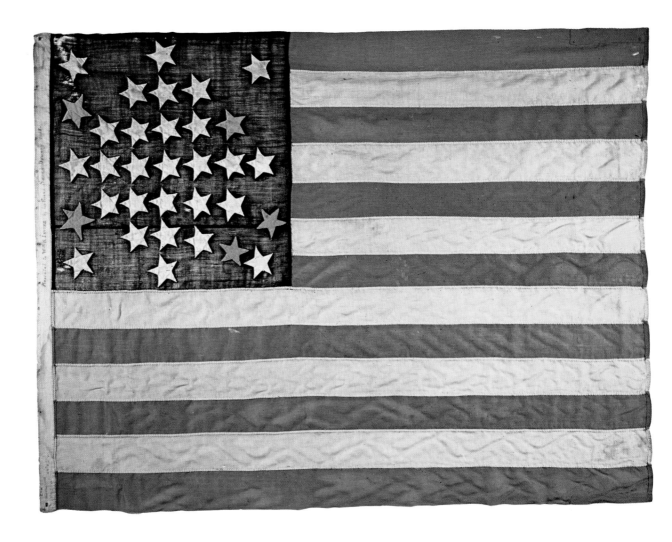

26 *William Neill Irvine Flag, Diamond Pattern.* 1847. Bunting. 44 x 60 in.

67 *First Confederate Flag, dated Savannah, May, 1861.* 1861. Bunting. 27 x 36 in.

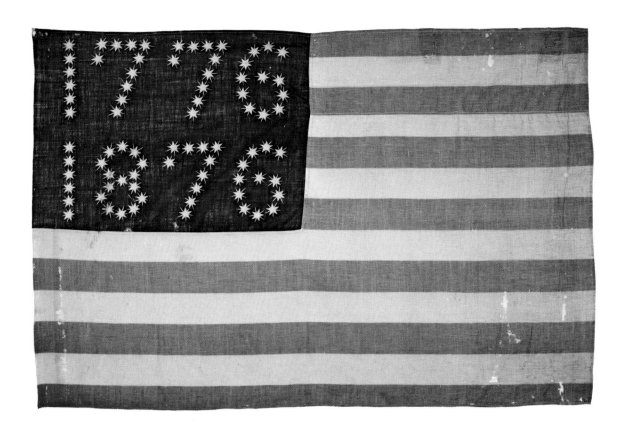

73 *1776-1876 Centennial Flag.* 1875. Printed glazed muslin. 28 x 43 in.

107 *General George McClellan's Presidential Campaign Flag,*
"George Brinton Mc.Clellan". 1864. Embroidered silk, 17¾ x 24 in.

120 *America*. 1801. Hand-colored mezzotint. 10 x 14 in.

126 *Children's Flag.* 1861-65. Silk with gold stars. 6¾ x 11 in.

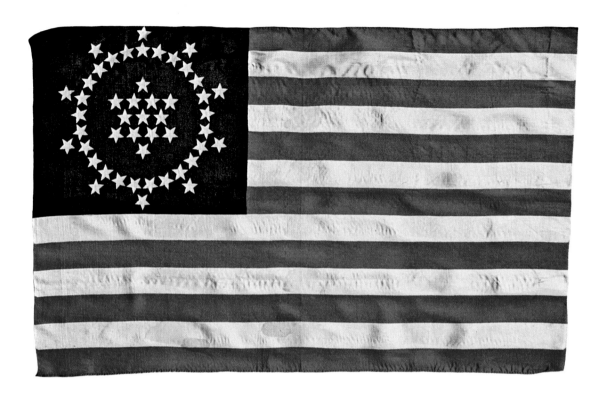

144 *"Peace Flag", designed by Wayne Whipple.* 1912. Printed silk. 15 x 24 in.

Monochrome Plates

30

1 *Apotheosis of Benjamin Franklin.* c. 1785. English cotton. 30 x 33 in.

2 *United States Customs Flag.* c. 1890. Bunting. 72 x 120 in.

5 *Medallion Motive for Know-Nothing Flag.* c. 1850. Roll-printed cotton. 17¾ x 21¾ in.

6 *See Our Torn Flag.* 1844. Hand-colored engraved music sheet. 13¼ x 10⅛ in.

8 *Washington Medal.*
1883. Aluminum. 1⅝ in. diameter.

12 James Smillie, *Hoisting the Flag at the Battery, New York, Nov. 25, 1783.* 19th century. Ink wash on paper. 4¼ x 6¾ in.

13 *Oval Wreath Flag, after Pierre L'Enfant design* c. 1783-95. Silk. 21¼ x 33¼ in.

15 *Revolutionary Flag, Third Maryland Pattern.* c. 1781-95. Bunting. 20½ x 25¼ in.

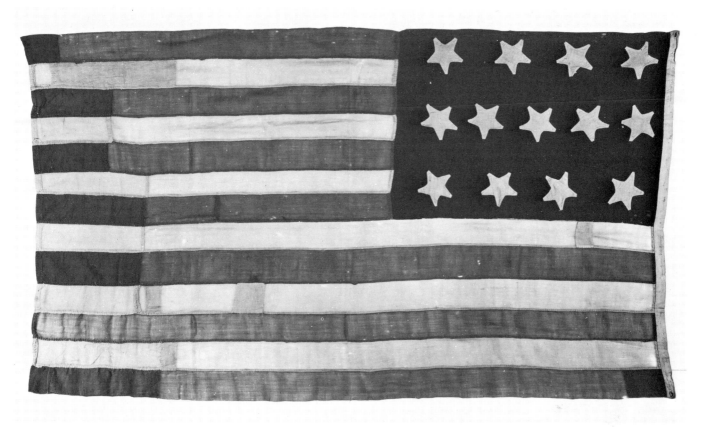

19 *Revolutionary Flag Belonging to John Spear of the Privateer* Minerva *(Front).* c. 1780-90. Bunting. 48 x 88 in.

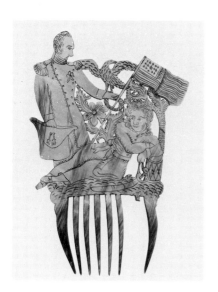

21 *High Comb with Lafayette and Star-Spangled Banner.*
c. 1810-1818. Turtle shell. 8⅞ x 6¼ in.

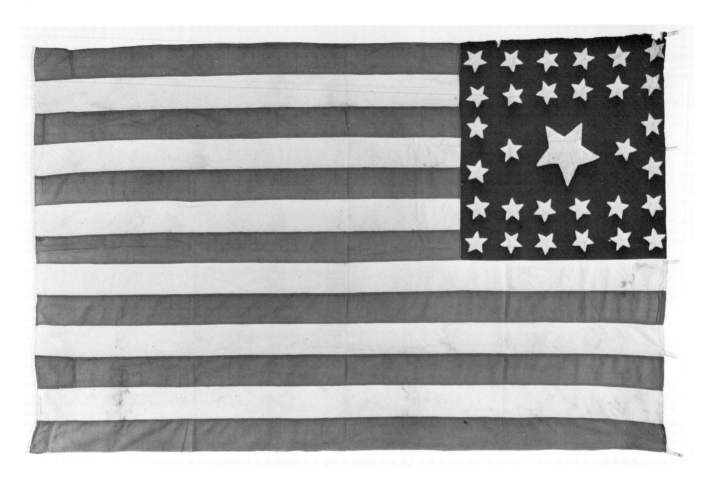

27 *Square Frame Flag.* 1851. Bunting. 44 x 70 in.

28 *Columbia*. 1873. Hand-colored lithograph. 22 x 19 in.

37 *The Kingsboro Flag, signed, HOLMES.* 1838. Wool and painted cotton. 72 x 174 in.

42 *Great Star Flag from Vermont.* 1837. Printed cotton. 12½ x 17 in.

43 *Great Star Flag.* 1837. Printed silk. 19½ x 28 in.

46 *Umbels, or Snowflakes, Flag (Detail)*. 1861. Bunting. 69 x 111 in.

51 *Double Wreath Medallion Flag (Detail)*. 1867. Bunting. 168 x 264 in.

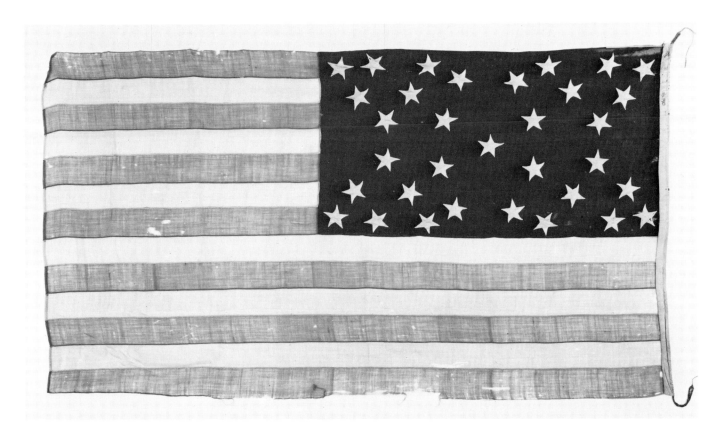

52 *Parentheses, or Butterfly, Flag.* 1859. Bunting. 72 x 126 in.

63 *Great ''L'' Regimental Flag.* 1861. Printed silk with oil painting and fringe. 30 x 43 in.

65 *Contest Model for Confederate Flag.* 1861. Cotton. 36 x 60 in.

66 *Contest Model for the Stars and Bars.* 1861. Cotton. 12 x 36 in.

68 *Regimental Confederate Flag, ''God Armeth the Patriot.''*
1861. Wool crêpe and satinette. 34 x 65 in.

69 *Confederate Flag with central ''Virginia Star.''* 1861. Bunting. 54 x 114 in.

77 *Centennial Flag.* 1876. Printed glazed muslin. 10½ x 15 in.

80 *Centennial Fan. Copyright Model dated 1875.* 1875. Hand-colored woodcut on Japanese paper and bamboo. 20¾ in. wide when open.

81 *Philadelphia International Exhibition Flag of French Manufacture.*
1875. Double weave silk. 3 x 5½ in.

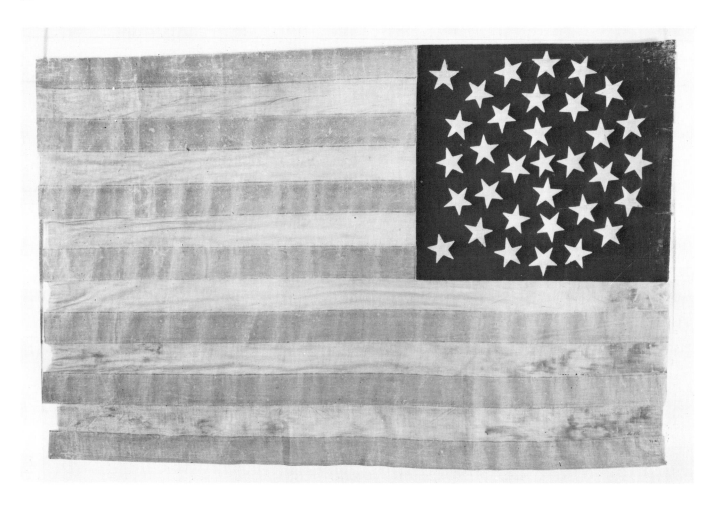

83 *Centennial Flag, Global Pattern.* 1876. Printed glazed muslin. 26x 43 in.

88 *Petit Point Needlebook.* 1845. Wool. 2 x 4 in.

89 *Needlecase Flag.* 1865. Wool. 2½ x 4 in.

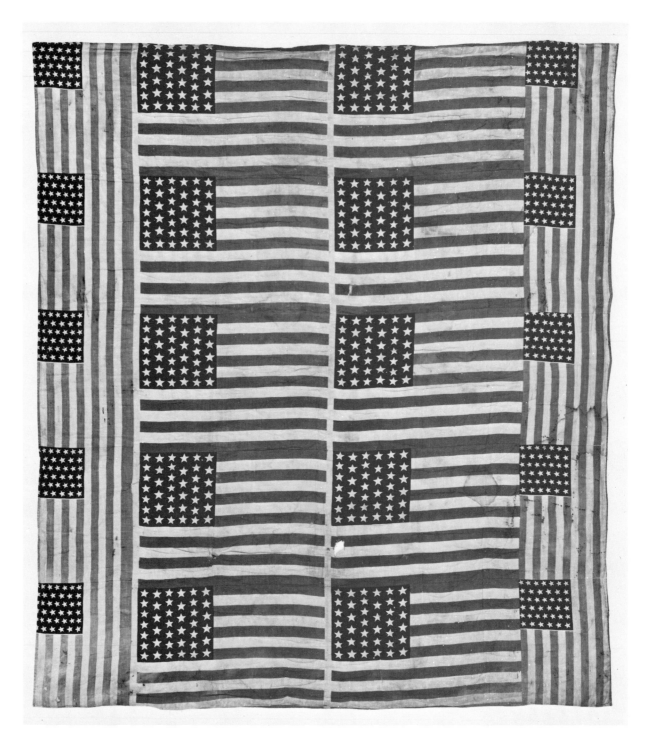

97 *Flag Quilt with Reverse of International Centennial Flags.* 1876. Cotton. 78 x 72 in.

125 Louis Icart, *Miss America*. 1927. Hand-colored etching. 28 x 20½ in.

127 *Children's Flag.* 1861-65. Silk with silver stars. 6 x 10 in.

128 *Children's Flag.* 1861-65. Silk with silver stars. 6 x 12 in.

129 *Children's Flag with Advertising Text, "Don't Cook in Warm Weather."* c. 1876. Printed paper. 4¾ x 8 in.

139 *Admiral Dewey Commemorative Banner
Inscribed "The Hero of Manila."*
1898. Printed cotton. 23¼ x 25½ in.

148 *Washington Guards Eagle Standard (Reverse).* 1838. Oil on silk. 42 x 48 in.

157 *Grand Union Flag (Replica).* c. 1876. Printed cotton. 17 x 26 in.

The Exhibition

1 *Apotheosis of Benjamin Franklin*
c. 1785. English cotton. 30 x 33 in.

2 *United States Customs Flag*
(13 stars, 16 stripes). c. 1890. Bunting. 72 x 120 in.

3 *Know-Nothing Flag*
(17 stripes, initialed and dated). 1858. Cotton. 19 x 24 in.

4 *Know-Nothing Keepsake*
1855. Book. 7¾ x 5¼ in.

5 *Medallion Motive for Know-Nothing Flag*
c. 1850. Roll-printed cotton. 17¾ x 21¾ in.

6 *See Our Torn Flag*
(26 stars, 9 stripes). 1844.
Hand-colored engraved music sheet. 13¼ x 10⅛ in.

John L. Magee
7 *Death of George Shifler*
1844. Hand-colored lithograph. 15 x 10¼ in.

8 *Washington Medal*
1883. Aluminum. 1⅝ in. diameter.

9 *Revolutionary Blue Stars Flag,*
Hand-lettered band added for Presidential campaign of 1880
(13 stars, 12 stripes). c. 1780-90. Wool and cotton. 60 x 114 in.

10 *Antique Pennant*
(3 stars). c. 1820-40. Wool and silk. 9 x 12 in.

11 *Antique Pennant*
(1 star). c. 1820-40. Wool and silk. 9 x 13 in.

James Smillie
12 *Hoisting the Flag at the Battery, New York, Nov. 25, 1783*
19th century. Ink wash on paper. 4¼ x 6¾ in.

13 *Oval Wreath Flag, after Pierre L'Enfant design*
(13 stars, 13 stripes). c. 1783-95. Silk. 21¼ x 33¼ in.

14 *Kirby Flag*
(13 stars, 13 stripes). c. 1780-90. Bunting. 30 x 40 in.

15 *Revolutionary Flag, Third Maryland Pattern*
(13 stars, 13 stripes). c. 1781-95. Bunting. 20½ x 25¼ in.

16 *Twenty-Star Flag*
(20 stars, 13 stripes). 1818. Bunting. 57½ x 104 in.

17 *Hubbard Flag*
(17 stars, 13 stripes). 1803. Bunting. 32 x 48 in.

18 *Naval Pattern Flag, Quincuncial Pattern*
(13 stars, 9 stripes). c. 1780-90. Bunting. 33 x 39 in.

19 *Revolutionary Flag Belonging to John Spear*
of the Privateer Minerva
(13 stars, 13 stripes). c. 1780-90. Bunting. 48 x 88 in.

20 *The Prisoner's Flag*
(13 stars, 13 stripes). c. 1777-1795.
Wool twill and silk. 8½ x 13½ in.

21 *High Comb with Lafayette and Star-Spangled Banner*
(15 stars, 15 stripes). c. 1810-1818.
Turtle shell. 8⅞ x 6¼ in.

Matthias Sprengel
22 *Pocket Book Almanac*
1784. Book. 5 x 3⅛ in.

23 *Mary Eliza Pennant*
(28 stars, 6 stripes). 1846. Bunting. 96 x 240 in.

24 *Thirteen-Star Pennant*
(13 stars, 2 stripes). c. 1840-50. Bunting. 240 in.

25 *Seaman's Chest Cover*
1854. Polychrome wood. 16 x 31 in.

26 *William Neill Irvine Flag, Diamond Pattern*
(33 stars, 13 stripes). 1847. Bunting. 44 x 60 in.

27 *Square Frame Flag*
(31 stars, 13 stripes). 1851. Bunting. 44 x 70 in.

28 *Columbia*
1873. Hand-colored lithograph. 22 x 19 in.

29 *Scatter Design Flag*
(31 stars, 13 stripes). 1851. Bunting. 47 x 70 in.

30 *War Stripe Flag*
(33 stars, 13 stripes). 1859. Wool crêpe. 34½ x 50 in.

Bass
31 *Antique Flag Sheet*
1837. Hand-colored engraving. 20 x 25 in.

32 *Monitor Hooked Rug*
1862. Cotton. 33½ x 57 in.

Attributed to John Bellamy
33 *Carved Flag and Jack*
c. 1889. Polychrome wood. 21 in. high.

34 *Naval Jack*
(39 stars). c. 1876-1889. Printed cotton. 12½ x 12½ in.

35 *Confederate Bible Flag*
(13 stars, 3 bars). 1865. Silk with paper stars. 5¼ x 9¾ in.

36 *The Liberty Eagle*
c. 1800. Oil on canvas. 35 x 46½ in.

37 *The Kingsboro Flag, Signed HOLMES*
(26 stars, 13 stripes). 1838. Wool and painted cotton. 72 x 174 in.

38 *Sanitary Fair Exposition Eagle*
1864. Wool and silk needlepoint with medal beading. 13 x 12 in.

39 *Chinese Embroidery Eagle*
c. 1890. Silk. 19½ x 22½ in.

40 *Alaskan Memento from Unalakleet*
1911. Beadwork on elk leather. 17 x 18 in.

Schuyler Hamilton
41 *The History of the National Flag of the United States of America*
1853. Book. 7⅞ x 5⅛ in.

42 *Great Star Flag from Vermont*
(26 stars, 13 stripes). 1837. Printed cotton. 12½ x 17 in.

43 *Great Star Flag*
(26 stars, 13 stripes). 1837. Printed silk. 19½ x 28 in.

44 *Great Star Flag*
(33 stars, 13 stripes). 1859. Printed silk. 8 x 11 in.

45 *Giant Great Star Flag*
(26 stars, 13 stripes). 1837. Bunting. 14 x 19 in.

46 *Umbels, or Snowflakes, Flag*
(34 stars, 13 stripes). 1861. Bunting. 69 x 111 in.

47 *Ensign of the schooner* United States, *Hayes Arctic Expedition*
(18 stars, 13 stripes). 1860. Cotton. 24 x 36 in.

48 *Lincoln Mourning Flag*
(36 stars, 13 stripes). 1865. Silk with crêpe border. 22½ x 34 in.

49 *Franco-Anglo-American Peace Flag*
(48 stars, 13 stripes). 1918. Printed silk. 12 x 17 in.

50 *Western Pioneer Flag of the Dodge Family*
(33 stars, 10 stripes). 1859. Cotton. 80 x 171 in.

51 *Double Wreath Medallion Flag*
(37 stars, 13 stripes). 1867. Bunting. 168 x 264 in.

52 *Parentheses, or Butterfly, Flag*
(33 stars, 13 stripes). 1859. Bunting 72 x 126 in.

53 *Windblown Flag*
(36 stars, 13 stripes). 1865. Bunting. 36 x 60 in.

54 *Bad Kissingen Flag*
(44 stars, 13 stripes). 1891. Printed silk. 18 x 24 in.

55 *Hourglass Flag*
(38 stars, 13 stripes). 1867. Bunting. 72 x 126 in.

56 *Fifty-Four Star Flag*
(54 stars, 13 stripes). 1912. Bunting. 58 x 99 in.

57 *Civil War Ensign, Phalanx Pattern*
(34 stars, 13 stripes). 1861. Bunting. 102 x 216 in.

58 *Civil War Flag*
(36 stars, 13 stripes). 1865. Printed silk. 13 x 15½ in.

59 *Great Erie Flag*
(35 stars, 13 stripes). 1865. Bunting. 360 x 516 in.

60 *Gildersleeve Meteor Flag*
(26 stars, 13 stripes). 1837. Bunting. 114 x 208 in.

61 *Sunshade*
(36 stars, 14 stripes). 1861-65.
Wood, metal and printed cotton. 20 in. high.

62 *The Old Flag of the War 1861-65*
(13 stars, 13 stripes). 1865. Bunting. 48 x 88 in.

63 *Great "L" Regimental Flag*
(34 stars, 13 stripes). 1861.
Printed silk with oil painting and fringe. 30 x 43 in.

64 *Open Center Flag*
(34 stars, 13 stripes). 1861. Bunting. 34 x 44 in.

65 *Contest Model for Confederate Flag*
(13 stars, 7 stripes). 1861. Cotton. 36 x 60 in.

66 *Contest Model for the Stars and Bars*
(13 stars, 3 bars). 1861. Cotton. 12 x 36 in.

67 *First Confederate Flag, dated Savannah, May, 1861*
(7 stars, 3 bars). 1861. Bunting. 27 x 36 in.

68 *Regimental Confederate Flag, "God Armeth the Patriot"*
(12 stars, 3 bars). 1861. Wool crêpe and satinette. 34 x 65 in.

69 *Confederate Flag with central "Virginia Star"*
(11 stars, 3 bars). 1861. Bunting. 54 x 114 in.

70 *Colonel Ellsworth*
1861. Colored lithograph. 13 x 9½ in.

71 *Death of Colonel Ellsworth*
1861. Hand-colored lithograph. 14 x 10 in.

72 *Confederate Banner*
(11 stars). 1861-65. Wool. 29 x 60 in.

73 *1776-1876 Centennial Flag*
(81 stars, 13 stripes). 1875. Printed glazed muslin. 28 x 43 in.

74 *Centennial Flag*
(38 stars, 13 stripes). 1875. Printed glazed muslin. 16 x 24 in.

75 *Centennial Banner with Portrait of Washington*
(36 stars, 13 stripes). 1875. Printed glazed muslin. 42 x 28 in.

76 *International Centennial Flag*
(39 stars, 13 stripes). 1875. Printed cotton. 16½ x 24 in.

77 *Centennial Flag*
(13 stars, 13 stripes). 1876. Printed glazed muslin. 10½ x 15 in.

78 *Centennial Flag for California*
(31 stars, 13 stripes). 1876. Printed glazed muslin. 22 x 36 in.

79 *Centennial Souvenir Bandanna*
1875. Cotton. 20½ x 26 in.

80 *Centennial Fan, Copyright Model dated 1875*
1875. Hand-colored woodcut on Japanese paper and bamboo.
20¾ in. wide when open.

81 *Philadelphia International Exhibition Flag*
of French Manufacture
(36 stars, 13 stripes). 1875. Double weave silk. 3 x 5½ in.

82 *Double Oval-Wreath Centennial Flag*
(38 stars, 13 stripes). 1877. Bunting. 72 x 138 in.

83 *Centennial Flag, Global Pattern*
(33 stars, 13 stripes). 1876. Printed glazed muslin. 26 x 43 in.

84 *Confederate Ensign, Double Crescent Pattern*
(11 stars, 3 bars). 1861. Cotton. 13 x 21¼ in.

85 *Double-sided Game Board*
c. 1835. Polychrome wood. 19 x 19 in.

86 *Flag Print Kerchief*
1862. Cotton. 17½ x 37½ in.

87 *Petit Point Flag with Glass Staff*
(34 stars, 13 stripes). 1861. Wool with silk lining. 1½ x 2¾ in.

88 *Petit Point Needlebook*
(27 stars, 13 stripes). 1845. Wool. 2 x 4 in.

89 *Needlecase Flag*
(36 stars, 13 stripes). 1865. Wool. 2½ x 4 in.

90 *Pair of Tapestry Flags*
(34 stars, 13 stripes). 1861. Wool needlepoint. 2½ x 4 in.

91 *Clock Dial*
(32 stars, 13 stripes). c. 1860. Leaded glass. 18 in. diameter.

92 *Carved Centennial Flag*
(38 stars, 13 stripes). 1876. Polychrome wood. 12½ x 17 in.

93 *Ambrose Knapp Advertising Flag*
(13 stars, 13 stripes). 1876. Printed glazed muslin. 4½ x 6¾ in.

94 *Johnson Book Store Advertising Card*
(38 stars, 13 stripes). c. 1890. Printed paper. 5 x 2½ in.

95 *Magnolia Ham Advertisement*
1878. Colored lithograph. 3½ x 5 in.

96 *Centennial Kerchief*
(39 stars, 13 stripes). 1876. Cotton. 17⅛ x 16⅝ in.

97 *Flag Quilt with Reverse of International Centennial Flags*
(39 stars, 13 stripes). 1876. Cotton. 78 x 72 in.

98 *Cotton Centenary Apron*
1890. Cotton. 35⅓ x 32½ in.

99 *Grand Army of the Republic Plaque*
(38 stars, 13 stripes). 1876. Hand-painted slate. 8½ x 14 in.

100 *German Box*
c. 1912. Brass and enamel. 2¾ in. diameter x 1 in. high.

101 *Japanese Box*
c. 1912. Silver and enamel. 2⅛ in. diameter x 2⅛ in. high.

102 *Old Glory Embroidery*
1890. Cotton. 18 x 17 in.

Currier and Ives
103 *Grand, National, Whig Banner*
1852. Hand-colored lithograph. 13½ x 9¼ in.

104 *Campaign Flag, "Our Policy the Will of the People"*
(34 stars, 13 stripes). 1861. Bunting. 240 x 360 in.

105 *Campaign Flag, "Equal Taxation,"*
Double Wreath Medallion Pattern
(37 stars, 13 stripes). 1868. Bunting. 228 x 288 in.

106 *General George McClellan's Presidential Campaign Flag,*
"God and My Country"
(35 stars, 13 stripes. 1864. Embroidered silk. 17¾ x 24 in.

107 *General George McClellan Presidential Campaign Flag,*
"George Brinton Mc·Clellan"
(35 stars, 13 stripes). 1864 Embroidered silk. 17¾ x 24 in.

108 *Tammany Hall, National Convention, July 4, 1868*
1868. Colored lithograph. 15 x 19⅜ in.

109 *Blaine and Logan Campaign Flag*
(38 stars, 13 stripes). 1884. Printed silk. 15½ x 24 in.

110 *McKinley Campaign Banner*
(46 stars). 1896. Printed silk. 6 x 12 in.

111 *Washington and Hayes Commemorative Textile*
1889. Printed cotton. 24 x 24 in.

112 *Presidential Candidate's Baldric*
(13 stars, 3 stripes). c. 1880. Silver and velvet on silk. 41 x 5 in.

113 *Bandanna Inscribed*
"The Stars and Stripes Will Always Wave for Protection."
1888. Printed silk. 20 x 20 in.

114 *Benjamin Harrison Campaign Flag, Global Pattern*
(36 stars, 13 stripes). 1876.
Printed glazed muslin with cotton band. 13 x 23 in.

115 *Harrison and Morton Campaign Ribbon Flag*
(30 stars, 13 stripes). 1888. Silk. 2½ x 4 in.

116 *McKinley and Hobart Flag Pin*
1896. Metal. 1¼ x 1½ in. when open.

117 *Circular Fan*
(13 stars, 13 stripes).
c. 1890. Gouache on paper. 23½ in. diameter.

118 *Harrison and Morton Campaign Scarf*
1888. Printed silk. 19 x 19 in.

119 *Harrison and Morton Campaign Flag*
Inscribed "Protection & Prosperity."
(288 stars, 13 stripes). 1888. Cotton. 54 x 36 in.

120 *America*
1801. Hand-colored mezzotint. 10 x 14 in.

121 *America*
1803. Hand-colored mezzotint. 9¼ x 7¼ in.

122 *Columbia with Flag of 26 Stars*
1837. Hand-colored lithograph. 10 x 7 in.

Currier and Ives
123 *The Star-Spangled Banner*
c. 1850. Colored lithograph. 13½ x 9½ in.

124 *Washington Memorial*
1800. Painted silk with chenille embroidery. 16½ x 21½ in.

Louis Icart
125 *Miss America*
1927. Hand-colored etching. 28 x 20½ in.

126 *Children's Flag*
(13 stars, 13 stripes). 1861-65. Silk with gold stars. 6¾ x 11 in.

127 *Children's Flag*
(32 stars, 13 stripes). 1861-65. Silk with silver stars. 6 x 10 in.

128 *Children's Flag*
(indeterminate number of stars, 13 stripes).
1861-65. Silk with silver stars. 6 x 12 in.

129 *Children's Flag with Advertising Text,*
"Don't Cook in Warm Weather"
(13 stars, 13 stripes). c. 1876. Printed paper. 4¾ x 8 in.

130 *Children's Flag Inscribed "Susan Lucas Ward, July 4, 1872"*
(36 stars, 13 stripes). 1872. Printed glazed muslin. 6½ x 9½ in.

131 *Children's Flag Inscribed "Martha Ward, July 4, 1872"*
(36 stars, 13 stripes). 1872. Printed glazed muslin. 6½ x 9½ in.

132 *Wheeler & Wilson Advertising Card* (Little Betsy Ross)
c. 1890. Colored imprint. 5⅜ x 2⅛ in.

133 *Admiral Dewey Comemorative Toy Drum*
1898. Wood, leather, rope and painted tin.
12 in. diameter x 8½ in. high.

134 *Rachel Albright Flag* (Grandaughter of Betsy Ross)
(13 stars, 13 stripes). 1904. Silk. 11 x 19½ in.

135 *Patriotic Belle*
1908. Chromolithograph on canvas. 22⅛ x 23 in.

136 *Forty-Two Star Flag* (unofficial)
(42 stars, 13 stripes). 1889. Cotton. 37 x 62 in.

137 *Lotus Club Flag*
(44 stars, 13 stripes). 1904. Watercolor on paper. 15½ x 19½ in.

138 *Chinese Brooch with Flag*
(48 stars, 13 stripes). 1912. Silver filigree and enamel. 1½ x 1 in.

139 *Admiral Dewey Commemorative Banner*
Inscribed "The Hero of Manila."
1898. Printed cotton. 23¼ x 25½ in.

140 Victor Gillam, *"Our Flag"*
c. 1918. Colored lithograph. 24 x 36 in.

141 *Flag Kerchief*
(128 stars, 39 stripes). c. 1910. Printed silk. 11½ x 11½ in.

142 *American History Quilt*
c. 1890. Cotton. 102 x 69 in.

143 *Great Star Bandanna*
(41 stars). 1889. Printed cotton. 22⅛ x 24¼ in.

144 *"Peace Flag,"* designed by Wayne Whipple
(48 stars, 13 stripes). 1912. Printed silk. 15 x 24 in.

145 *Shield*
(13 stars, 13 stripes)
c. 1880. Paper maché. 19 x 15¾ in.

146 *Walking Cane with Flag*
(39 stars, 13 stripes). c. 1876.
Wood and printed cotton. 34½ in. long.

147 *Patriotic Cyclist*
c. 1890. Hand-colored photograph. 14¾ x 10⅞ in.

148 *Washington Guards Eagle Standard*
1838. Oil on silk. 42 x 48 in.

149 *Illustrated Civil War Envelopes* (eight)
1861-65. Printed paper. Approximately 4¾ x 5½ in.

J. Drake
150 *Document Signed by Thomas Jefferson with Flag Vignette*
of six-pointed "Flaming" Heraldic Stars
1808. Engraving on parchment. 16⅞ x 14¼ in.

151 *An Emblem of America*
1798. Hand-colored mezzotint. 10 x 14 in.

152 *Civil War Canteen With Thirteen Star Flag*
1861. Tin. 8 in. diameter.

153 *Washington Memorial Textile*
1819. Printed cotton. 26 x 19 in.

154 *Campaign Scarf Inscribed "Protection to American Industry"*
(38 stars, 13 stripes). c. 1876. Silk. 16 x 16 in.

155 *Great Flower Flag*
(34 stars, 13 stripes). 1861. Bunting. 108 x 132 in.

156 *Huntington Flag*
(13 stars, 13 stripes). 1777-95. Bunting. 34¾ x 59¾ in.

157 *Grand Union Flag* (Replica)
(13 stripes). c. 1876. Printed cotton. 17 x 26 in.

Henry Bill
158 *"Flag Sheet"*
1848. Colored lithograph. 19 x 23 in.

159 *Flag Cards* (four)
1880-1901. Printed paper. Approximately 3 x 5 in.

160 *Assemblage of Twenty-two Miniature Flags,*
two Frontal Bosses and one Hat Pin
including numbers 81, 87, 90 and 115.

BOOK DESIGN AND PRODUCTION: RYA/CRAWFORD DUNN, INCORPORATED, DALLAS
TYPOGRAPHIC COMPOSITION: TEXT — SOUTHWESTERN TYPOGRAPHICS INC., DALLAS   COVER — TYPOGRAPHICS COMMUNICATIONS INC., NEW YORK
COLOR SEPARATIONS: COURTESY OF ALFRED A. KNOPF, INC., NEW YORK
LITHOGRAPHY: MOTHERAL PRINTING COMPANY, FORT WORTH
BINDING: JOHN D. ELLIS BINDERY, DALLAS

TYPE FACES: LINOFILM HELVETICA — TEXT, 9 ON 13 WITH 30 POINT BOLD INITIAL;   RUNNING HEADS, 24 POINT LIGHT;
QUOTATIONS, 8 ON 11 LIGHT;   CAPTIONS, 7 ON 8;   COVER, EGIZIO AND HELVETICA BLACK
COVER PAPER: CHAMPION'S, 10-POINT CAST-COATED, KROMEKOTE
TEXT PAPER: NOTHWEST'S, 100-LB., DULL ENAMEL, VINTAGE
END PAPER: FOX RIVER'S, 65-LB. COVER, BERRY BLUE, MODIVATION